# Georgian
# BATH

# Georgian
# BATH

PAT DARGAN

AMBERLEY

First published 2012

Amberley Publishing
The Hill, Stroud
Gloucestershire, GL5 4EP

www.amberleybooks.com

British Library Cataloguing in Publication Data.
A catalogue record for this book is available from the British Library.

ISBN 978 1 4456 0959 1

Typeset in 10pt on 12pt Sabon.
Typesetting and Origination by Amberley Publishing.
Printed in the UK.

# CONTENTS

# GLOSSARY OF TERMS

| | |
|---|---|
| Arch | A semi-circular or curved head that spans a doorway or window. |
| Architrave | The decorated frame around a doorway or window opening. |
| Area | The small basement-level yard at the front of a house. |
| Balustrade | A low barrier or screen made up of pedestal-type uprights. |
| Base | In a Classical context, the squat decorated bottom part of a column. |
| Basement | The floor of a building that lies below the ground level. |
| Bays | The divisions of an elevation by regular spaces such as windows or columns. |
| Block | A group of terraced houses taken together. |
| Capital | The decorated top of a Classical column. |
| Classical | The style of Greek or Roman architecture. |
| Column | A circular or square pillar divided into three sections – base, shaft and capital. |
| Cornice | The decorated moulding positioned at the junction of a wall and ceiling. |
| Doorcase | The main entrance to a Georgian house including the door, the surround and the fanlight. |
| Elevation | The front, back and sides of a building. |
| Entablature | A decorated beam spanning between Classical columns. |
| Fanlight | A semi-circular window over a door. |
| Georgian | Period in history corresponding approximately to reign of Georgian monarchs in Britain. |
| Jamb | The flat inner edge of a door or window opening. |
| Lintel | A horizontal beam that spans an opening. |
| Niche | A tall round-headed space built into a wall. |

| | |
|---|---|
| Palace-fronted Block | A block of terraced houses built so as to appear as a single palace-type building. |
| Parapet | A low protective wall built along the edge of a roof. |
| Pediment | The triangular gable over a bay, doorway or window. |
| Piazza | An enclosed square or similar open space. |
| Plot | The individual building site on which a Georgian house and garden was laid out. |
| Portico | An open porch comprising a row of columns and a triangular pediment-type roof. |
| Renaissance | Historical and artistic period approximately between the fourteenth and seventeenth centuries. |
| Rustication | The emphasised horizontal and vertical lines of masonry joints. |
| Sash | The opening part of a window. |
| Shaft | The tall main circular part of a column. |
| String Course | A projecting horizontal band built into a wall. |
| Terrace | A row of houses linked together in the form of a single block. |
| Closing Vista | The formal view of an architectural feature that closes the end of a street. |

# 1
# THE GEORGIAN
# IDEAL

## Introduction

The City of Bath is located in the South West of England, about twenty kilometres inland from the port of Bristol where, during the eighteenth century, or Georgian period, it experienced a period of dramatic expansion, when an extensive range of uniform streets, landscaped spaces, blocks of tall stone-built Georgian houses, and public buildings made their appearance. Such was the extent and success of these developments, that Bath can be ranked firmly amongst the upper echelons of Britain's Georgian cities. In 1987 UNESCO acknowledged this when it marked the development of the city as a masterpiece of human creative genius.

This guide for the general reader sets out to explore the Georgian aspect of Bath, introduces the individuals who contributed to its creation, examines the ideas and influences that motivated and inspired them, and presents an outline of their achievements. In this context it is worth noting that the term 'Georgian' refers to the historic period that corresponds to the reign of the Georgian monarchs on the British throne, approximately between 1700 and 1800. The hope of the guide is to introduce the history, form and force that is Georgian Bath. Before exploring these achievements though, it is worth pausing to consider the main ingredients that lay at the heart of, and underpinned, all Georgian town developments in the British Isles including Bath.

## Estate Development

The practice of eighteenth-century town development first emerged in seventeenth-century London when the Earl of Bedford wished to develop his lands at Covent Garden in London for housing. New developments in London were prohibited at this time, but Lord Bedford secured permission from the Crown to do so in 1630 for a fee of two thousand pounds. As part of his approval, he was obliged to trust the design of his proposal to the king's architect: Inigo Jones. Jones's proposal went on to become the first Renaissance urban development to be completed in Britain and it consisted essentially of laying out an Italian style piazza. This was a central public open area around which were built a series of terraced houses. The design of the square and the houses was based on Italian Renaissance town planning ideals, which Jones may have seen on his visits to Italy. In spatial terms, the Covent Garden piazza consisted of a rectangular square entered through four access roads (Fig. 1). Both the north and east side of the piazza had large blocks of terraced houses that fronted onto the roadway, while on the east side, St Paul's church was flanked on each side by single blocks of houses. Lord Bedford's gardens lay to the south and initially this remained free of development.

The impact of Lord Bedford's development at Covent Garden was considerable and almost immediately other landowners across the city launched similar development proposals. These were all given blocks of terraced houses, arranged around central squares like Covent Garden. These developments, however, differed in one important aspect from the Covent Garden model, in that the open piazza was replaced by a central landscaped garden, which was reserved for the exclusive use of the square's residents.

In 1661 the Earl of Southampton began to develop his lands in Bloomsbury, where he devised a simple system to assist with the legal and financial aspects of the development process. Up to this point, most landowners could not sell or subdivide their estate lands without an Act of Parliament, which could only be achieved through considerable delay and at great cost. Lord Southampton sidestepped this difficulty by setting out the lines of the house plots on the ground and then leasing these to builders by the means of a building lease. Southampton received a yearly rent from the leaseholder, but he retained control of the house design through the terms of the lease. Later when the lease expired, the house and site reverted back to the estate. Just as the concept of the Covent Garden residential square became popular; the Southampton lease system was soon taken up and used by other developing landowners around London.

The layout of the narrow building plots also emerged during this period. In these cases, the house plots were arranged in rows along the new streets, or around the new squares. This allowed the landowner to squeeze the maximum number of houses into the minimum of road frontage and at the same time achieve the maximum profit from the leasing of the land. This was extremely advantageous to the landowner. He risked little, as his investment was small. He rarely became involved in the building process and his only outlay was for the construction of roads and services. He collected yearly rents over the period of the lease, and on the expiry of the lease the entire property reverted back to his ownership. The house builder on the other hand risked all. He paid for the construction of the house and he had to wait until he successfully sold on the lease of the completed house before he realised his profit.

## The Terraced House

When Jones laid out his houses in Covent Garden he modelled the elevations on the ideas of the Italian Renaissance architect Palladio. This Palladian style of architecture, as it came to be known, was based on the Classical temple fronts of ancient Greece and Rome and stood on a raised base, or plinth. On top of this was a row of tall Classical columns, with a decorated beam or entablature stretched along the tops of the columns. Generally, but not always, the entablature carried a large triangular panel, or pediment. For this reason the architecture of the eighteenth century is often referred to as Classical or Palladian. Jones followed these Palladian principles in the elevation of St Paul's church in Covent Garden. Here the formal base was not included and four Classical columns and the overhead entablature stretched across the front of the church. Above this a large triangular pediment, the full width of the building, was constructed (Fig. 2).

In the case of the house block elevations, Jones followed the Palladian principles, although the triangular pediment was not included. A ground-level arcade of arches acted as the base. Above this the two upper levels were divided into bays by full-height Classical columns. In addition, a window was placed between the columns on each floor level (Fig. 3). In effect, each block of terraced houses resembled an Italian Renaissance palace and in this way the concept of the central square and the palace-fronted housing blocks was introduced to London and became a model for later developments.

Today, the layout of the Covent Garden piazza survives, but nothing remains of Jones's original houses. However, the design of Lindsey House in nearby Lincoln's Inn Fields, which dates from 1640, has been attributed to Jones and offers an early example of the use of the Palladian palace-fronted model (Fig. 4). Here the ground level arcade of arches, used in Covent Garden, was replaced by windows and the stone work at this level is rusticated. That is, the joints between the individual stones were deliberately exaggerated. Above this, the upper storeys were divided into bays by Classical columns, with a single window placed between each column – much the same as in Covent Garden. No pediment was included, but a decorated balustrade acted as a parapet and stretched across the roof line. At a later period Lindsey House was remodelled as two independent houses. Fortunately, the only disruption to the house front was the replacement of the original entrance by a pair of independent doors.

As the seventeenth century advanced, the standard Georgian terraced house gradually emerged. Initially these houses were three storeys high with a pair of rooms on each floor – one room to the front and one to the back. The ground-floor level held the living rooms, with the hall and stairs to one side, while above this the upper floors were used as bedrooms. Later a basement and attic storey was added, bringing the total number of floors to five. By 1700 the standard form and architecture of the Georgian street and square was complete. This included the railed central garden, the enclosing carriageway, the footpath, and the blocks of palace-fronted houses. It can be seen therefore that the prime ingredients in the development of Georgian London were profit to the landowner and builder and taste in the form of the Palladian Classical street architecture, and it was these same ingredients that influenced other improving landowners as a massive programme of urban development was initiated all across the country. Under a spirit of eighteenth-century optimism, new housing developments were laid out and existing areas were improved. Within this improving movement, tall elegant houses, wide boulevards, squares, crescents and elegant public buildings made their appearance. In the case of Bath, three individuals in particular influenced and guided the city's activities with outstanding results. These were Ralph Allen, Beau Nash and John Wood.

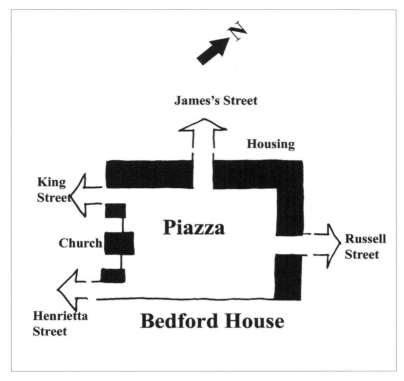

Fig. 1 Diagrammatic layout, Covent Garden, London.

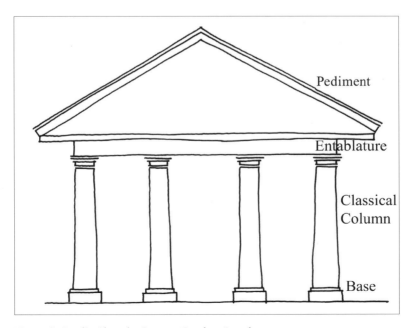

Fig. 2 St Paul's Church, Covent Garden, London.

*Left:* Fig. 3 Palace-fronted housing, Covent Garden, London.

*Below:* Fig. 4 Lindsey House, Lincoln's Inn Fields, London.

# 2
# SPACE & TIME

In the case of Bath, Ralph Allen was the economic power that drove the Georgian development of that city (Fig. 5). He was born in Cornwall in 1693 and initially worked as a Post Office clerk. He moved to Bath in 1710 and two years later, at the age of nineteen, he was appointed postmaster of the city. In 1720, at the age of twenty-seven, he took on the running of the postal system in the entire south-west of the country and over the next forty years went on to reform, rationalise and improve the system right across the North of England, in the process of which he earned a considerable fortune. In addition to his business interests Allen also involved himself in local politics. He was a member of Bath Council, was elected Mayor of the city in 1742, and he represented the city in the House of Commons between 1757 and 1764. In 1727 Allen purchased the nearby Combe Down Quarry, which produced a particularly warm-looking honey-coloured stone. Allen saw that the future development of Bath could offer considerable opportunity for his stone, particularly in the hands of the architect John Wood, whom Allen believed had the necessary vision and skill to help him exploit what is now referred to as Bath stone. In the event, the investment in the quarry proved an advantageous one, and as the development of Georgian Bath unfolded, the bulk of stone used came from Allen's quarries.

If Allen was the economic driver of Bath's success, Richard Beau Nash was the nucleus around which the social life of the city revolved. He was born in Carmarthen in Wales and came to Bath in 1703 with a career in law, military and gambling behind him (Fig. 6). He was appointed the city's Master of Ceremonies in 1704 and he set about improving the low levels of the city's social behaviour. He successfully introduced a formal code of civility and elegance that was enthusiastically embraced by the citizens of Bath and visitors alike. In this way he effectively controlled the running of Bath and established the city as a major centre of eighteenth-century British cultural and genteel living. Under his direction, the city's daily social life revolved around dining, bathing, gaming, music, dancing, and the theatre.

It was, however, the architect John Wood who played the major part in the physical development of Georgian Bath and his arrival in the city was, in all probability, prompted by the reputation of Allen and Nash. Wood was born in 1704 (Fig. 7), although where he received his training in architecture is not known. He seems to have worked in London around 1725 where he may have been familiar with the concepts and forms of the London developments such as Covent Garden and Grosvenor Square. Wood also worked in Yorkshire and it was here that he formulated his proposals for the development of Georgian Bath, inspired perhaps by his London experience.

## Place

When Wood arrived in Bath he found a city still in the Middle Ages. It was positioned on a bend on the River Avon, oval in shape, and still enclosed by its town walls (Fig. 8). Inside the walls lay a network of streets and lanes, with the four main thoroughfares leading to the North, South, East and West gates respectively. Today the town walls have mostly vanished, but their course remains marked by the lines of Upper and Lower Borough Walls. Outside the South Gate, the line of Southgate Street Road was lined with suburban houses and led to the bridge over the River Avon. Beyond the North Gate a second suburb had emerged where the line of the current Broad Street entered the city. Both the lands to the west and on both sides of the riverbank remained undeveloped.

## Space

Sometime around 1726 Wood acquired a map of Bath and began work on his proposal. This included the development of an area of undeveloped land that lay in the north-west corner of the city immediately beyond the city walls. He held some discussions with the landowner, Robert Gay, and he secured a lease to develop the lands, where he acted both as architect and developer. In 1726 he laid out Queen Square and succeeded in leasing out building plots to builders. The project seems to have been successful and Wood followed this by the laying out of Gay Street. This stretched northwards and uphill from the square, at the end of which he started work on the Circus in 1754. Here he arranged a sequence of terraced blocks around a circle. Unfortunately Wood never saw the project completed as he died shortly after work on the building started. The project was subsequently completed by Wood's son, of the same name, following which he himself went on to lay out the spectacular Royal Crescent in 1767.

During this same period a number of other developments were undertaken in the city. These were located both inside and outside the city walling – developments that incorporated new uniform streets as well as squares and crescents. Nor were the Woods the only architects successfully operating in Georgian Bath. For example, John Stratham was working on Beaufort Square, while John Eveleigh and John Palmer were concentrating their efforts on Camden and Lansdown crescents.

North of the Royal Crescent, St James's Square and a range of dramatically sited crescents filled the area between Cavendish Road and the banks of the Avon. Immediately south of the Royal Crescent was an extensive area of open parkland. Between the parkland and the river, work on a network of uniform streets and Norfolk Crescent was undertaken. This pattern of uniform streets continued around the south and south-east of the city walls as far as the Parades on the east bank of the Avon. In effect the Georgian extension of Bath consisted of an arrangement of streets, squares and crescents in a wide band that extended around the north, west, south and, to a lesser extent, the east side of the medieval city. Inside the town walls the medieval street pattern was largely retained although a number of new streets, such as Bath Street, were laid out. In addition, the older street architecture was gradually replaced by standard Georgian housing.

## Pace

Interestingly, there was no master plan for the development of Georgian Bath. The city just expanded piecemeal in the form of individual housing projects. These were linked together by connecting roads, but they were otherwise unrelated in spatial terms. The time-scale during which Georgian Bath emerged lasted for a little over seventy years. Queen Square and Beaufort Square were under-way by 1728. Work on the Circus and the Royal Crescent had started by 1770 and as 1790 approached Lansdown Crescent and Great Pulteney Street were under-way. Beau Nash had died in 1761. Richard Allen followed in 1764 and twenty-seven years later John Wood the younger joined them. As 1800 approached, the population of Bath was approaching 40,000 and the maximum point of the city's Georgian expansion had been reached (Fig. 9). At this stage, the line of the Lansdown Crescent complex formed the northern boundary. Cavendish Road and Marlborough Buildings formed the western boundary, while the area between the Lower Borough Walls and the river was gradually filled in. The River Avon had restricted development to its western bank, except for the completion of the single Great Pulteney Street development on the east bank. By this period, the popularity of Bath as a leisure and health centre had begun to decline. The city ceased to attract the previous levels of residents and visitors and after this date little fresh development was contemplated. The physical form of Georgian Bath was effectively complete. Today the great bulk of Georgian Bath survives intact except in the area south of Lower Borough Walls and the Henry Street. Here the street pattern survives, but unfortunately the eighteenth-century fabric gave way to later developments.

   The work of the Woods, both father and son, as well as the other architects and developers, left the City of Bath with a remarkable legacy of eighteenth-century town planning and architecture. The variety, originality and richness of the spatial forms, the skilful application of the palace-fronted ideals, and the consistency of the Bath stone, all produce a masterful townscape of elegant boulevards, landscaped squares, and splendid crescents. Before considering the elements of this legacy in detail, however, it is appropriate to take a closer look at the standard Georgian house of the period – the basic architectural unit of eighteenth-century Bath.

*Above left:*  Fig. 5  Ralph Allen.

*Above right:*  Fig. 6  Richard Beau Nash.

*Right:*  Fig. 7  John Wood.

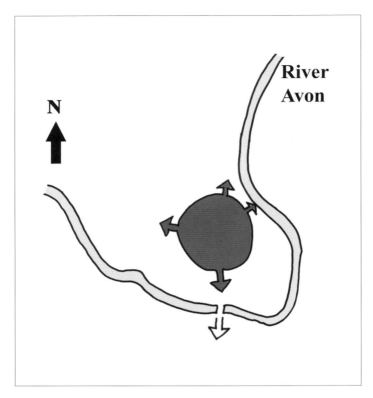

Fig. 8  Plan of Bath
*c.* 1700.

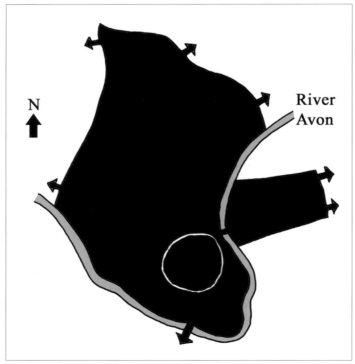

Fig. 9  Plan, Bath *c.* 1800.

# 3
# THE GEORGIAN HOUSE

## Internal Arrangements

The Georgian houses of Bath were built primarily to cater for the needs of the aristocratic or wealthy occupiers, who flocked to the attractions of the city and the spa. Generally the internal layout of the house followed the standard London double room arrangement, with the kitchen and servants' quarters in the basement, the dining and reception rooms on the ground and first floors and the bedrooms on the upper floors (Figs 10 & 11). The main staircase of the house started in the hall at ground level and usually stopped at the second-floor level. Above this, the top storey in the attic was reached by means of a small stairs tucked into one corner. Here the floor was often divided into four small rooms for the use of the children or servants. In a number of cases these standard arrangements were altered by the Bath builders, to conform to the wishes of the individual owners. Annexes of different forms and sizes were often added to the rear of the houses to increase the accommodation. In other instances, two houses were combined into single dwellings, although the original elevation of the pair was left in place to conform to the uniformity of the terrace, as was the case in some of the houses in the Royal Crescent.

The relationship between the street level, the ground-floor level and the garden level can be confusing and relates to the way the houses were built. The basement was the first level of the house to be completed and it was built at the natural ground level. The road level was then gradually built up so that the road level and path surface matched the ground-floor level of the house. Above this the remaining floors were completed at different levels. An open area was left immediately at the front of the house onto which the basement windows opened. In addition, a store was often built under the footpath and this opened off the area. Access to the main door was then provided by a short bridge over the area and both the bridge and the area itself were protected by a cast iron railing (Fig. 12). Inside the house, the floor-to-ceiling heights of the rooms varied from floor to floor. The dining and living rooms on the ground and first floor were given the highest ceilings. The second and third floors were lower, while the basement and the attic rooms were lower still. The decoration of the houses followed a similar pattern, with the more important rooms having the most impressive decoration. The ground- and first-floor rooms had ornate plasterwork ceilings with elaborate cornices and ceiling roses, as well as fine joinery, panelled doors, window shutters and an elegant staircase. The level of decoration decreased in the less important rooms, such as the bedrooms, and was non-existent in the kitchens. The basic construction of the houses consisted of Bath stone walling which carried the wooden floors, while overhead the pitched roof was tiled or slated and partially hidden from the street by front parapets.

## Elevations

One of the most distinguishing features of the Bath houses is the combination of Bath stone and the use of the Palladian-style elevations. Generally, the architectural treatment fell into two categories: Palladian and plain. The former was based on that introduced by Jones in London, and included the rusticated ground level, the division of the upper levels into bays by double-storey classical columns, as well as the decorated cornices and triangular pediments. The houses on Queen Square, for example, all successfully display these Palladian features in their elevations (Fig. 14). In the case of the plain elevations, the rustication, columns, cornices, and pediments were discarded, so that the house front consisted of the flat Bath stone front, relieved only by the vertically proportioned windows and doorways. The houses in Great Pulteney Street, for example, were all given this type of plain elevational treatment (Fig. 13).

In both the Palladian and plain categories the practice of grouping the houses into palace-like blocks continued, except where the site conditions, such as steep slopes, made this impossible.

Occasionally the plain type of elevation was augmented by the inclusion of a triangular pediment at roof level, such as Duke Street (Fig. 15). This served to emphasise the idea of the palace-fronted block. Another feature on the elevations of the Bath houses worth noting is the street signs, which frequently appear high up on the end of blocks or on corner houses. These gave the name of the street, or individual terrace block, and consisted of precise Roman lettering skilfully cut into the stonework, such as in Bedford Street (Fig. 16).

## Windows

As a rule, the windows of the Bath Georgian houses were vertically proportioned, with heights that relate to the ceiling heights of the rooms they served. As the heights of the rooms varied, so also did the window heights. The first-floor windows are the highest, the ground- and second-floor windows are lower, and the third and basement windows lower still, all echoing the hierarchical nature of the various floors. The number of windows on each of the upper floors of the houses reflects the scale of the interiors. The more modest houses have two windows, or bays, per floor (Fig. 17). The wider houses have three bays (Fig. 18); while the largest houses were given four or five bays. These same patterns were repeated in the attic windows in the roof.

The windows themselves consisted of vertical sliding sashes, each of which was divided into small panes by narrow glazing bars (Fig. 19). Each sash was given three horizontal panes, while the number of vertical panes varied from six to two – depending on the window height. This characteristic feature of most Georgian houses was essentially a cost factor, driven by the fact that the small panes of glass were less expensive than larger ones. There were however a small number of variations to the standard window. In a number of houses in Brock Street (Fig. 20) and St James's Parade, for example, the rectangular windows were replaced by a Venetian-type design. In these cases, each window was given three separate openings set closely together, where the central opening was wider than the outer ones and was given a semi-circular head. In other cases, such as in Great Pulteney Street, the windows were given semi-circular heads.

## Doors

The doorcases of the Bath houses were generally modest affairs and consisted of a single door set into a wooden frame with a rectangular window on top to allow light into the hall (Fig. 21). In a number of instances the overhead window was more elaborate and was given a semi-circular or fanlight shape (Fig. 24). In the large houses the door was set into a formal doorcase frame. This often took the shape of a miniature Classical temple front with Classical side columns and a triangular pediment (Fig. 22).

## Ironwork

Occasionally, such as in Gay Street, St James's Square, and Great Pulteney Street, cast iron balconies were introduced at the upper levels (Fig. 23). These are not balconies in the true sense, but box-frames that were bolted to the wall at the base of the first-floor windows. Other examples of cast ironwork frequently found outside the houses were foot scrapers and lamp holders. The foot scrapers were positioned immediately outside the entrance doors and were provided to facilitate the scraping of mud from footwear before the wearer entered the house (Fig. 26). The design consisted essentially of a low-level horizontal blade that was supported between a pair of decorated legs. In a number of instances, such as Lansdown Crescent and Great Pulteney Street, the houses were given arched lamp holders. Here lamp holders were positioned at the crown of elaborately decorated metal arches that spanned across entrance steps (Fig. 27). Elsewhere in a simpler arrangement, the lamp was positioned on a decorated arm that projected out from the wall face (Fig. 28). Another metalwork feature occasionally found on one side of the entrance door is the candle snuffer (Fig. 29). This has a cone-shaped funnel that allowed a person to extinguish a taper or a candle.

## Shop Fronts

Before moving on to explore the street and spatial elements of Georgian Bath it is worth noting the impact of retailing on some of the Georgian houses, particularly in Milsom Street and Old Bond Street. In such cases the ground floor of the house was changed from residential to retail use. A large opening was made in the front wall at street level and a shop front was inserted. This usually consisted of a single- or double-glazed window, a doorway, and an overhead sign board, or fascia. These could be plain rectangular or elaborately curved forms such as those in Old Bond Street (Fig. 25).

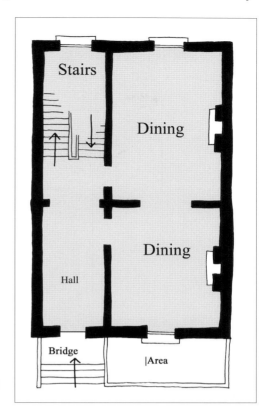

Fig. 10 Ground-floor plan, standard terraced house.

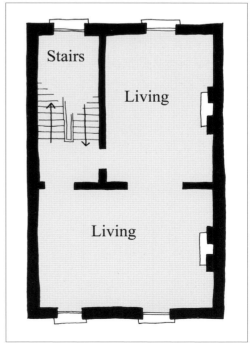

Fig. 11 First-floor plan, standard terraced house.

Fig. 12  Bridge and area, Queen Square.

Fig. 13  Plain-fronted elevation, Great Pulteney Street.

Fig. 14  Palladian palace-fronted elevation, Queen Square.

Fig. 15 Central pediment in plain elevation, Duke Street.

Fig. 16 Street sign, Bedford Street.

Fig. 17 Typical two-bay house.

Fig. 18
Typical
three-bay
house.

*Right:* Fig. 19  Standard Georgian window.

*Below:* Fig. 20  Venetian window, Brock Street.

*Above left:* Fig. 21 Standard door.

*Above right:* Fig. 22 Temple-front doorcase.

*Right:* Fig. 23 Balcony.

*Below:* Fig. 24 Semi-circular fanlight.

Fig. 25  Shop fronts, Old Bond Street.

*Top right:* Fig. 26  Foot scraper.

*Top left:* Fig. 27  Arched lamp-holder.

*Bottom left:* Fig. 28  Wall-mounted lamp.

*Bottom right:* Fig. 29  Wall-mounted candle snuffer.

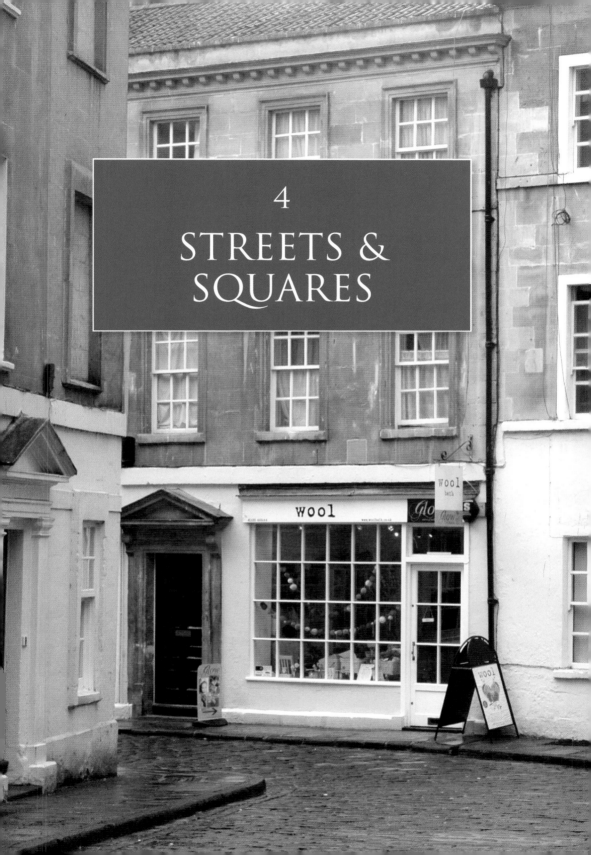

# 4
# STREETS & SQUARES

## The Uniform Street

The uniformly laid out streets are undoubtedly the most common elements of Georgian Bath with numbers that exceed two hundred, from the thirty-metre-wide Great Pulteney Street to the much narrower New Bond Street. The uniform street is essentially a formal piece of urban design that includes a carriageway of a standard width that is flanked on either side by a footpath. Inside the footpath, the palace-fronted house blocks were laid out to a uniform building line, with the basement open area at the front and long narrow gardens at the rear. At the ends of the gardens it was not uncommon to have a coach house that opened onto a narrow service lane, or mews, that stretched along the rear of the plots. Two examples demonstrate the characteristic layout of the typical Bath street: Great Pulteney Street and the Parades.

In most cases the houses of Georgian Bath are merged together in the form of palace-fronted blocks. The significance of this is that the houses should be viewed not as individual dwellings but as aspects of a uniform street-scape. This was not always the case, however, particularly where the houses were built on hilly sites, such as Gay Street or Marlborough Buildings. In these instances the terraced blocks were laid out to a fixed building line (Fig. 30), but the idea of the uniform palace-front was lost as the levels of the individual houses rose in a series of steps in line with the rise of the street levels (Fig. 32). In the medieval sector of the city between the Upper and Lower Borough Walls, the complex ownership of the properties was not conducive to the laying out of long palace-fronted blocks. In these cases, the pre-eighteenth-century buildings were gradually replaced by individual Georgian houses, as and when the properties changed hands or when old leases expired. This often resulted in street-scapes with irregular lines and mixed house-fronts, such as in Pierrepoint Place (Fig. 33).

Great Pulteney Street offers a powerful example of the unified street-scape. Here a sequence of regular blocks was laid out along the wide carriageway on the east side of the River Avon by the architect Thomas Baldwin. The central block of terraced houses is shown in Figure 31, as well as the two blocks on the far side of the roadway. The south-side block has thirteen houses with long gardens and a mews lane at the rear. The illustration also shows the lines of the carriageway, the footpath and the basement areas. The house elevations are plain and three bays wide (Fig. 34) except for the central house, which is considerably wider with five bays. Directly across the street the two blocks on the northern side are separated from one another by a roadway that leads to Pulteney Mews which stretches along the back gardens of the houses.

The Parades lies on the western edge of the city, between Pierrepoint Street and the east bank of the River Avon. The project was laid out in 1740 by John Wood senior and consists of two blocks of plain terraced housing (Fig. 35), set between North Parade and South Parade. The smaller block backs onto the river and has thirteen houses. Two houses face onto North Parade, five houses face onto Duke Street, which separates the two blocks, and six houses face onto South Parade. The back gardens of the houses extend to the river's edge and the houses have no rear service lane or mews. The large block between Duke Street and Pierrepoint Street has twenty-seven houses laid out on a tight square arrangement (Fig. 36). The short rear gardens all interlock together and again no service lane or mews was provided.

## The Garden Squares

When John Wood laid out Queen Square in 1727, he based it on the standard London model. The block on the north side of the square was given the full Palladian treatment, with a rusticated ground floor, Classical columns and a projecting central bay topped by a triangular pediment (Fig. 37). This treatment was abandoned in the other blocks and they were given the basic plain treatment (Fig. 38). All four blocks faced onto the central garden and were given long, narrow back gardens (Fig. 39), although only the north and west blocks were served by mews lanes. The central garden is enclosed by metal railings and the square is entered at each of the four corners by a pair of access roads. These are arranged at right angles to one another so that the square is entered from the sides. In 1738 a tall, needle-like obelisk was erected in the middle of the central garden at the instigation of Beau Nash. This created a kingpin effect, around which the space and architecture seem to be arranged.

Three other garden squares also made their appearance in Bath: Beaufort Square, St James's Square and Catharine Place. Beaufort Square is a little to the south of Queen Square, although it is much smaller in scale. It was laid out around 1727 by the architect John Stratham and consists of a small, railed central garden with a block of individual terraced houses on three sides (Fig. 40). The remaining south side was taken up by the Theatre Royal. The houses are all laid out to a uniform building line, but no effort was made to establish a uniform palace front. Instead the terraces were made up of two-, three- and four-storey houses arranged along the blocks.

St James's Square seems to date from around 1730 and was given a more formal and complex arrangement. It is rectangular in shape and larger than Queen Square. It has the usual railed central landscaped garden with the uniform blocks of plain housing arranged around it (Fig. 41). The most unusual feature of the square is the access roads, which are arranged so as to enter the square diagonally at the four corners (Fig. 42). Catharine Place is another small square that lies near the east side of the Royal Crescent. It consists of a narrow central garden with the entrance positioned at the four sides, although only the houses on the long side of the square were provided with rear service lanes (Fig. 43).

In addition to the rectangular-shaped squares, there are a number that were laid out around triangular greens. These include Queen's Parade, Green Park and Portland Parade. Queen's Parade lies at the north-west corner of Queen Square, and is spatially linked to it. It consists of a single block of plain houses facing onto the small, landscaped green area. An unusual feature of the block is that the houses were all given projecting front porches. Green Park, in the south-eastern corner of the Georgian city, originally consisted of two blocks of plain houses facing one another across a triangular green, with rear service lanes. Unfortunately the block on the east side no longer exists, although the surviving block and the green remain intact. In a different sequence, Portland Place was established by arranging the housing blocks at the junction of Portland Place and Burlington Street into a triangular space and providing a small green as a centrepiece (Fig. 44).

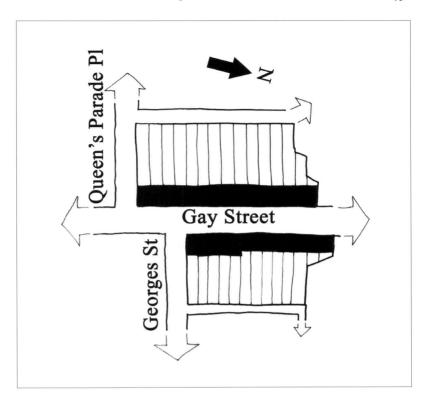

Fig. 30
Diagrammatic
layout, Gay
Street.

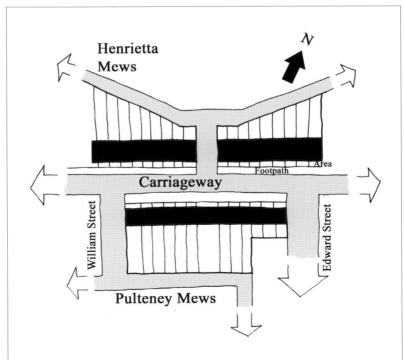

Fig. 31 Layout,
Great Pulteney
Street.

Fig. 32 Marlborough Buildings.

Fig. 33  Pierrepoint Place.

Fig. 34  Housing block, Great Pulteney Street.

Fig. 35  Housing, Duke Street, South Parade.

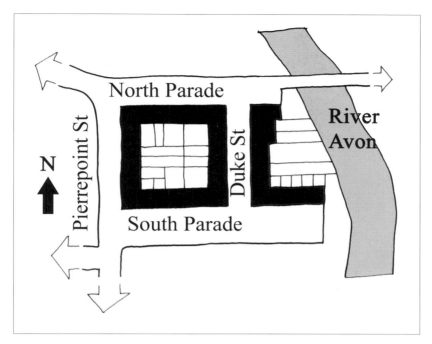

Fig. 36  Layout, The Parades.

Fig. 37  House block, north side, Queen Square.

Fig. 38  House block, east side, Queen Square.

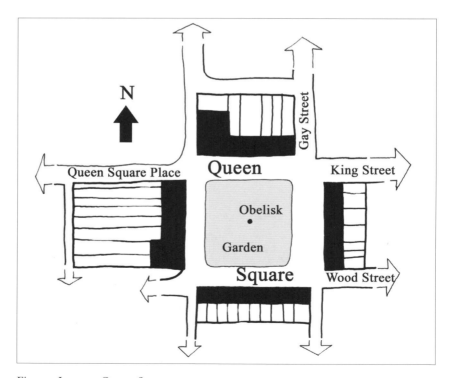

Fig. 39  Layout, Queen Square.

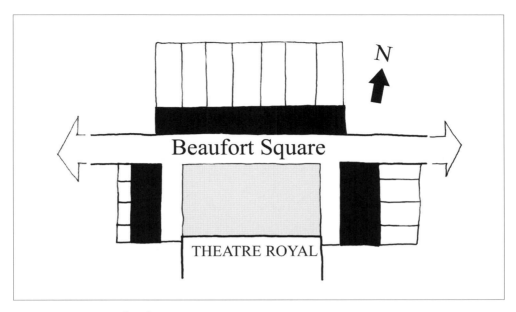

Fig. 40 Layout, Beaufort Square.

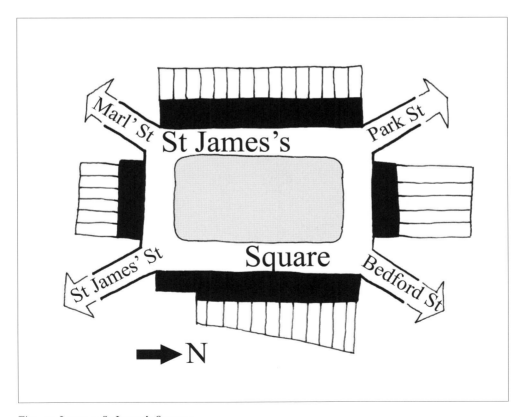

Fig. 41 Layout, St James's Square.

Fig. 42 Terraced housing block, St James's Square.

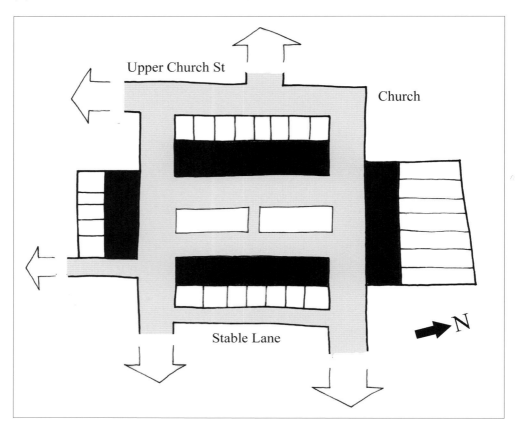

Upper Church St

Church

Stable Lane

N

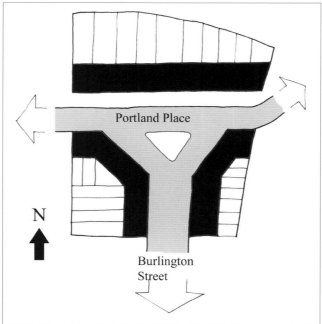

Portland Place

N

Burlington
Street

*Above:* Fig. 43 Layout,
Catharine Place.

*Left:* Fig. 44 Layout, Portland
Place.

5

# THE CIRCLE &
# THE CRESCENT

The use of the uniform street and the garden square in the early stages of Bath's Georgian development followed the conventional ideals of eighteenth-century town planning and street architecture. This limited repertoire was, however, extended when the Woods – father and son – introduced new urban spatial elements, first in the laying out of the Circus and subsequently when the perfection of the Royal Crescent was achieved.

## The Circus

When John Wood laid out the Circus in 1754, he abandoned the London garden square model and laid out three housing blocks in a curved arrangement around a circular open space. This space was initially a paved water cistern, but this was later removed and the current open landscaped garden was laid out. In the designing the Circus, Wood was responsible for the creation of one of the most notable examples of Georgian town planning in Britain. Here Wood set out Gay Street, Brock Street and Bennett Street so that they extended outwards from the centre of the circle, with the housing blocks set between each of the roads (Fig. 45). What emerged was essentially three crescent-shaped blocks arranged to form a circle (Fig. 46), outside of which a system of irregular planned mews lanes were provided.

In the case of the house design, Wood successfully adapted the Palladian-style palace-fronted architecture of Jones and developed it further. He provided a continuous symmetrical elevation in all three blocks, with full-height paired columns and decorated horizontal bands or cornices that dramatically and visually linked the blocks together (Fig. 47). In effect, the entire composition merged into a circular form that is said to reflect the image of the Colosseum in Rome – only turned inside out. Unfortunately, Wood died shortly after work started on the Circus and the operation was taken over and completed by his son – also John Wood. As an element of urban planning, the circular arrangement of the Circus was eminently successful. Curiously it was never repeated in Bath, although it later became a standard planning feature elsewhere such as in London and Edinburgh.

## The Royal Crescent

Further uphill, John Wood the younger developed the crescent idea further in 1767. He reverted to the Palladian-style palace-fronted elevation of Jones (Fig. 48), but instead of repeating the circular plan of the Circus, he laid out his thirty houses in the form of an extended elliptical crescent (Fig. 50). The houses were supplied with long rear gardens, behind which ran a service lane. In doing so, Wood introduced the crescent form of terraced housing into British town planning for the first time. In another novel move, Wood took advantage of the sloping site to introduce a significant element of landscape into the project. The line of the carriageway was set out to follow the elliptical curve of the crescent and the houses were built on one side of the road only (Fig. 51). On the far side of the road an extensive area of parkland was laid out on the grounds, which gently sloped downwards from the crescent. In this way, the houses were given extensive views of open landscape over the Avon valley.

In a further move, Wood built the front wall of the crescent in its entirety. He then leased out the otherwise vacant building plots to individual builders who were responsible for the design and construction of their own houses. Consequently, behind the image of the vast unified crescent, lies a range of different houses (Fig. 52). Notwithstanding this, Wood's handling of the form of the crescent and its elevational treatment is unquestionably the outstanding example of a Georgian streetscape in the British Isles. Despite this success, Wood played no part in the development of the other crescents in Bath, which included the extensive Lansdown Complex, as well as the individual Cavendish, Camden and Norfolk crescents.

## Lansdown Crescent Complex

In terms of breadth of scale and visual impact, Lansdown Crescent Complex is without parallel anywhere in the British Isles. It consists of a series of four individual terrace blocks and a roadway that follow a sloping serpentine course, stretching from Somerset Place in the north-western corner of Georgian Bath, south-eastwards as far as Lansdown Road (Fig. 53). The individual blocks are not physically linked, except for the two middle terraces, but visually merge together into a single unit and like the Royal Crescent, each of the blocks faces onto a landscaped parkland. The individual blocks generally follow the usual pattern of plain elevations, long rear gardens and mews service lanes.

The line of the complex begins at Somerset Place, followed in turn by Lansdown Place West, Lansdown Crescent, and Lansdown Place East (Fig. 53). Somerset Place was designed by John Eveleigh and work started in 1793, when he laid out the crescent of sixteen houses in a gentle concave curve (Fig. 54). The most significant feature of the block is the pair of central houses that project slightly forward from the main building line. This projecting bay is dramatically emphasised by a semi-circular pediment at roof level, which has a curved break at the top, into which is set a tall urn (Fig. 55). The projecting bay was also given a central niche at first-floor level, immediately over side-by-side doorways. East of Somerset Place, Lansdown Place West consists of a convex stretch of nine plain-type houses that rise slowly with the ground in a sequence of steps (Fig. 56).

Further east, Lansdown Crescent was designed by the architect John Palmer. Work started here in 1789 and the curve of the twenty houses follows a concave line (Fig. 57). Like Somerset Place, Lansdown Crescent was given a central bay by projecting the two centre houses slightly forward (Fig. 49). In this case the side-by-side doorways were singled out for special treatment. These were set into a miniature temple-like doorcase, divided into three bays by the two doors and a central niche (Fig. 58). There is also a matching niche at the first-floor level. An interesting addition to both the Lansdown Place and Lansdown Crescent is the small double-storey link that joins the two blocks together. This was completed sometime in the 1820s and has a wide elliptical access arch at ground level and a single residential storey overhead. The little link is finished off with a series of urns and a balustrade at roof level.

The final crescent in the sequence, Lansdown Place East, is made up of a second convex of sixteen houses that follow the downward slope of the ground in a series of steps (Fig. 59). These are much smaller in scale than the houses in the other crescents – a feature reflected in the narrow plots and gardens. Otherwise they follow the standard plain elevational treatment.

Elsewhere in Bath, the form of Cavendish, Camden and Norfolk crescents follow a convex plan, front onto landscaped open areas, and all were provided with mews lanes. Camden Crescent and Norfolk Crescent have sixteen houses apiece (Fig. 60 and 61), while the smallest, Cavendish Crescent, has eleven houses (Fig. 62). Cavendish and Norfolk crescents were given plain elevations. Camden Crescent, on the other hand, was given the full Palladian arrangement with a rusticated ground floor, Classical columns and a decorated cornice (Fig. 63). In addition, the two central houses step forward to form of a projected bay. This has a dramatic triangular pediment at roof level, as well as semi-circular windows and door openings at ground level.

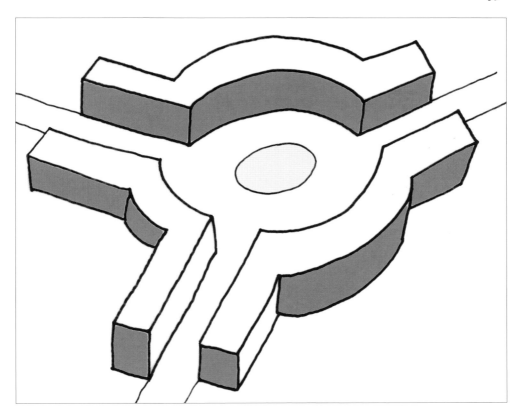

*Above:* Fig. 45 Diagrammatic
layout, the Circus.

*Right:* Fig. 46 Plan, the Circus.

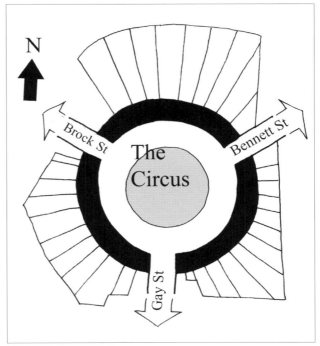

Fig. 47 Housing,
the Circus.

Fig. 48  House, the Royal Crescent.

Fig. 49  Central bay, Lansdown Crescent,
Lansdown Crescent Complex.

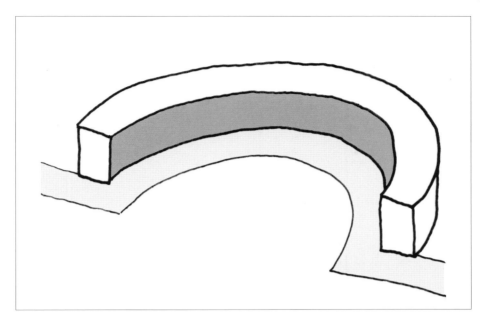

Fig. 50 Diagrammatic layout, the Royal Crescent.

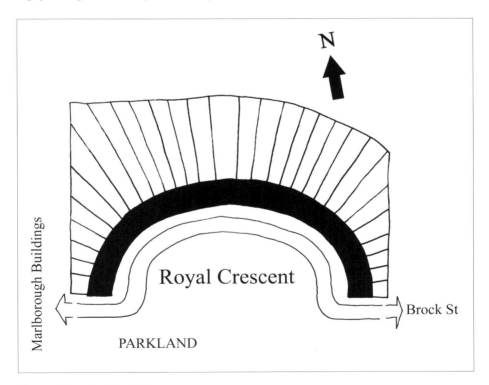

Fig. 51 Plan, the Royal Crescent.

Fig. 52 Housing, the Royal Crescent.

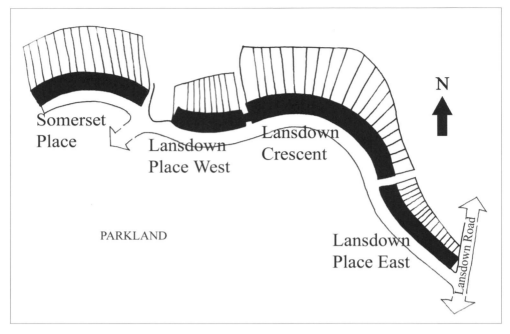

Fig. 53  Plan, Lansdown Crescent Complex.

Fig. 54
Housing,
Somerset
Place,
Lansdown
Crescent
Complex.

Fig. 55  Central Bay, Somerset Place,
Lansdown Crescent Complex.

Fig. 56  Housing, Lansdown Place West,
Lansdown Crescent Complex.

Fig. 57  Housing, Lansdown Crescent, Lansdown Crescent Complex.

Fig. 58
Doorcases, central
bay, Lansdown
Crescent,
Lansdown
Crescent
Complex.

Fig. 59 Housing,
Lansdown Place
East, Lansdown
Crescent
Complex.

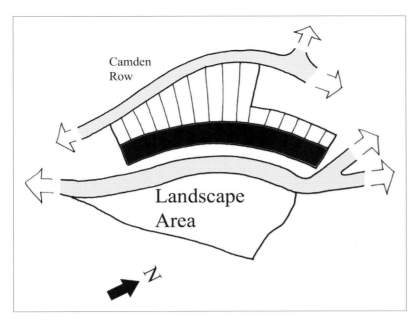

Fig. 60 Plan, Camden Crescent.

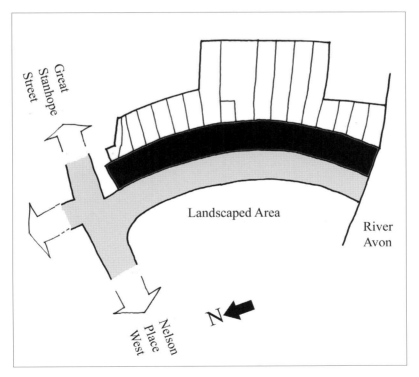

Fig. 61 Plan, Norfolk Crescent.

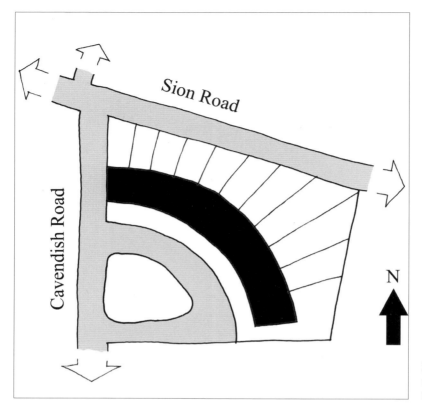

Fig. 62 Plan,
Cavendish
Crescent.

Fig. 63 Housing, Camden Crescent.

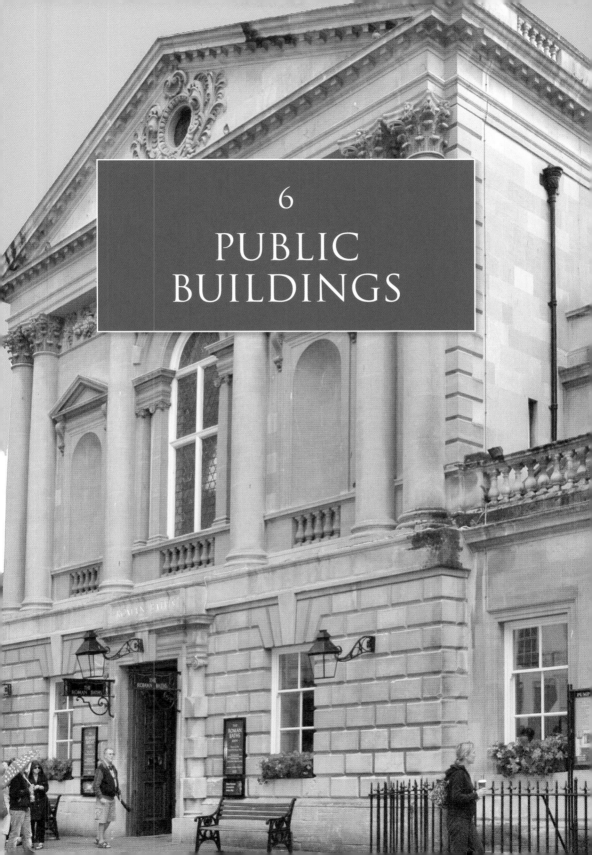

# 6
# PUBLIC BUILDINGS

In addition to the extensive range of Georgian houses, Bath has a number of eighteenth-century public buildings, mostly positioned within the old medieval city. The most significant of these includes the Grand Pump Room complex, the Upper Assembly Rooms, the Guild Hall, the Theatre Royal, and the Holburne Museum. All these were executed in Bath stone and all were completed in the Palladian style introduced by Inigo Jones. The extent and form of these public buildings warrants a separate publication. Consequently, the selected details presented here offer only a brief overview, sufficient to highlight their significance within Georgian Bath.

The Grand Pump Room complex consists of the Pump Room and the Concert Room, both of which face onto Abbey Church Yard, behind which are the Roman Baths and the Roman Baths Museum, with the latter facing onto Stall Street. The Grand Pump Room is a double-storey block with a basement and was designed initially by Thomas Baldwin in 1788, following which additions were later added by John Palmer. The building has an elegant central bay with a double-storey three-bay portico and an overhead pediment (Fig. 64). This is flanked on each side by a plain bay and a projecting end pavilion. The ground-floor windows are vertically proportioned, while the upper-level windows are small and elliptically shaped. The adjacent Concert Room elevation also has a double-storey with a rusticated ground level and a tall three-bay pediment overhead. The centre bay of the portico has a tall, rounded window with blank niches in the side bays (Fig. 65).

The Upper Assembly Room in Bennett Street, just off the Circus, consists of a three-storey block designed by John Wood the younger and dates from 1771. The elevation has mainly plain stonework with vertically proportioned windows and a roof line balustrade. The most notable feature is the single-storey western elevation. This has a central three-bay portico and pediment (Fig. 66). The porch is flanked on each side by a single window set into the solid masonry.

The Theatre Royal, designed by the architect George Dance the Younger, was laid out initially to front onto Beaufort Square in 1804. Today the building is much altered, although the Beaufort Square elevation survives intact (Fig. 67). This has a sequence of curve-headed windows at ground level. Above this, the double-storey upper level has its tall windows set between full-height Classical columns. The roof line is marked by stone lyres over the columns and a large central coat of arms.

The Guild Hall in High Street was designed by the architect Thomas Baldwin and opened in 1778. It is a three-storey block with its impressive elevation fronting onto the street (Fig. 68). This has a projecting central bay with a rusticated ground level and a double-storey portico and pediment overhead. The ground-level windows are round-headed, while those overhead are rectangular. The two side bays are the same height as the central bay, although the windows are arranged in a two-storey fashion. Here the windows are vertically proportioned, with the upper window set into a semi-circular arch.

The three-storey Holburne of Menstrie Museum at the end of Great Pulteney Street is one of the most significant of Bath's Palladian-style public buildings (Fig. 69). This has a central projecting bay flanked by two narrower side bays. The ground floor of the central bay is rusticated with three semi-circular arches. Above this is the tall three-bay portico and pediment, above which is the plain attic storey. The vertically proportioned first-floor windows are the tallest. The ground-floor windows are lower, while the attic windows are lower still.

Finally it is worth considering an example that is both a town planning feature and a public building: Pulteney Bridge. This remarkable combination of bridge and shopping parade was designed by the architect Robert Adam and was opened in 1774. Viewed from the bank the bridge spans the river in three semi-circular arches (Fig. 70). Above this the carriageway is lined on each side with an arcade of shops, with a central pavilion that incorporates a triangular pediment and a number of windows. This is flanked by four smaller projecting pavilions, each with a window and a small pediment. Two of these flank the main central pavilion, while the others were given small roof domes and mark the ends of the bridge. The double-storey shopping arcade at the street level has a row of small shops on each side of the carriageway. These have individual wooden shop fronts and vertically proportioned windows on the upper level (Fig. 71). On the south side of the carriage, the central pavilion has a large double-height window set within an arch, while the end pavilions were given similar but smaller windows. The end pavilions were also given small domed roofs. Across the carriageway the arrangement was simpler. This also has individual shop fronts, but the ends and centre point are marked only by slightly projecting bays with triangular pediments.

Fig. 64  Grand Pump Room, Abbey Church Yard.

Fig. 65 Concert Room, Abbey Church Yard.

*Above:* Fig. 66  Assembly Room, Bennett Street.

*Left:* Fig. 67  Theatre Royal, Beaufort Square.

Fig. 68  Guild Hall, High Street.

Fig. 69  Holburne of Menstrie Museum, Sidney Place, Great Pulteney Street.

*Above and below:* Figs 70 & 71 Pulteney Bridge.

# 7
# WALKING TRAILS

The most successful way to experience Georgian Bath is by following a walking trail through the streets, squares and crescents of the city. In this way it is possible to explore and absorb their history, planning and architecture at first hand. As the city is too extensive and complex for a single overall trail, three individual trails are offered: the Wood Family Trail, the Lansdown Crescent Trail and the Pulteney Bridge Trail. Each trail covers a specific aspect of Bath's Georgian planning and street architecture. The trail maps are supported by a series of short notes that highlight some of the significant points that may be of interest to the walker. The individual trails take about an hour to complete, although for the dedicated walkers, the three trails are located a reasonable distance from one another.

## Wood Family Walking Trail

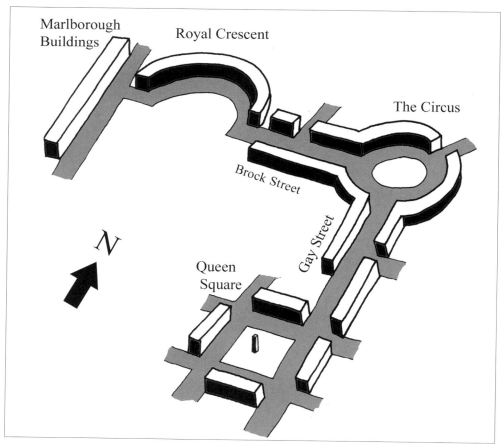

Fig. 72 Wood Family Walking Trail.

The Wood Family Trail highlights the major works of the Wood family: father and son. This starts at Queen Square and moves on to Gay Street, the Circus, Brock Street, the Royal Crescent and Marlborough Buildings (Fig. 72).

Start
Queen Square.
- Laid out by John Wood, 1728.
- First London-type square.
- Railed landscaped central garden.
- Central obelisk in garden.
- Four blocks arranged around garden.
- North block: Palladian-style block, three- and four-bay houses with central bay and end pavilions.
- East block: Plain block, five-bay houses.
- South block: Plain block, complex bay arrangement, central bay with pediment.
- West block: Part Palladian-style block, three- and four-bay houses, rusticated ground level, three projecting bays (Fig. 73).

From north side of Queen Square turn left into
Gay Street.
- Steep, sloping street laid out around 1740.
- Range of three blocks.
- Three-bay plain, individual stepped houses.
- Range of temple-front doorcases.

From Gay Street turn left into
The Circus.
- Laid out by John Wood, 1754.
- Circular central garden.
- Three crescent-shaped blocks.
- Outstanding three- and four-bay Palladian-style houses, with double Classical columns, decorated string courses, elaborate parapets with circular openings and overhead stone pineapples (Fig. 74).
- Some first-floor window boxes.

From the Circus turn left into
Brock Street.
- Laid out around 1760.
- Three plain blocks.
- Two- and three-bay houses.
- Projecting porches with temple-style doorcases.
- Number of houses with first-floor Venetian windows.

From Brock Street turn right into
The Royal Crescent.
- Laid out by John Wood the younger, 1767.
- Spectacular single crescent-shaped Palladian-style block (Figs 75 and 76).
- Three-bay houses.
- Balustrade-type parapet.
- Central house with side windows to doorcase and semi-circular window at first-floor level.
- Crescent overlooks landscaped parkland.

From the Royal Crescent turn left into
Marlborough Buildings.
- Extended block of plain stepped housing.
- Three-bay houses.
- Rusticated ground level.
- Mix of round- and square-headed windows.
- Some elaborate first-floor balconies.
- End of trail.

Fig. 73  East side, Queen Square.

Fig. 74 The Circus.

Fig. 75 Royal Crescent.

Fig. 76
Doorway,
Royal
Crescent.

## Lansdown Crescent Trail

The Lansdown Crescent Trail includes the most spectacular and inventive of Bath's crescents and landscapes. The trail begins at the junction of Cavendish Road and Sion Street and includes Cavendish Crescent, Somerset Place, Lansdown Place West, Lansdown Crescent, and Lansdown Place East (Fig. 77).

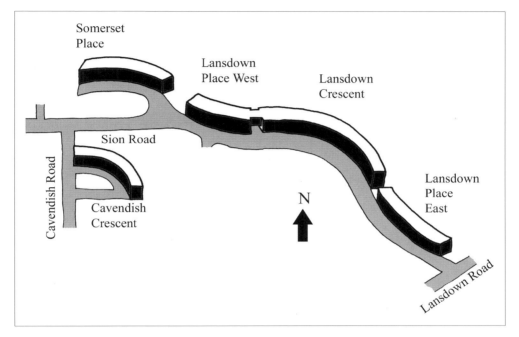

Fig. 77  Lansdown Crescent Walking Trail.

Start
At north end of Cavendish Road turn right into
Cavendish Crescent.
- Plain, three-bay houses (Fig. 78).
- String course with fourth-floor level over.
- Arched doorways.
- First-floor balconies.
- Crescent overlooks triangular green.

From Cavendish Crescent turn right into Cavendish Road, turn right into Sion Road, turn left into
Somerset Place.
- Laid out by John Eveleigh, 1793.
- Crescent of plain three-bay houses.

- Central projecting bay, with elaborate decorated circular pediment.
- Elaborate framed doorcases.
- First-floor string course.
- Some houses with balconies.
- Crescent overlooks oval landscaped garden.

From Somerset Place turn left into Sion Road as far as
Lansdown Place West.
- Laid out around 1790.
- Crescent Block of plain, three-bay stepped houses.

Continue along Sion Road to
Lansdown Crescent.
- Most elaborate crescent of the Lansdown complex.
- Laid out by John Palmer in 1789.
- Plain three-bay houses.
- Rusticated ground level.
- Central Palladian bay with Classical columns and pediment.
- Each end house given a projecting curved bay (Fig. 79).
- Arched lamp-holders.
- Balustrade-type parapet.
- Some wall-mounted candle snuffers.
- Elaborate central temple-type doorcase.
- Crescent overlooks landscaped parkland.

Continue along Sion Road to
Lansdown Place East.
- Laid out around 1790.
- Crescent block of plain, three-bay stepped houses.
- Some balconies on upper levels.
- Some temple-type doorcases.
- Crescent overlooks landscaped parkland.
- End of trail.

From the end of Lansdown Place West, it is possible to retrace the trail back to the
Royal Crescent, the Circus, and Queen Square. Alternatively, it is possible to turn right
into Lansdown Road and follow the road downhill into the main commercial and
shopping area of the city.

*Above:* Fig. 78  Cavendish Crescent.

*Right:* Fig. 79  Lansdown Crescent.

## Pulteney Bridge Trail

The Pulteney Bridge Trail includes the Georgian sector of Bath that lies on the east side of the River Avon. This was laid out by Thomas Baldwin and consists of Pulteney Bridge, Argyle Street, Laura Place, Great Pulteney Street, and Sidney Place, laid out in a straight axis between the bridge and Sidney Place (Fig. 80).

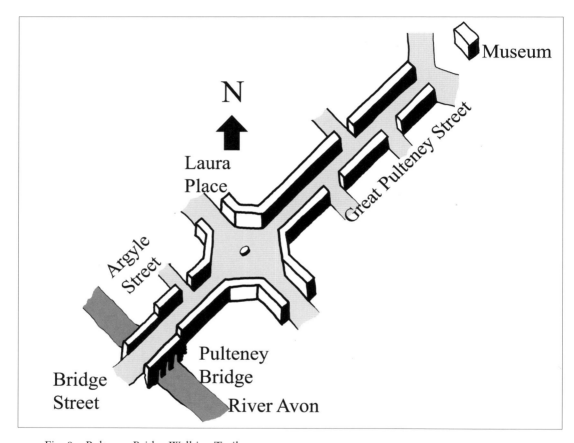

Fig. 80  Pulteney Bridge Walking Trail.

Start
Pulteney Bridge.
- Laid out by Robert Adam around 1770.
- Parade of shop fronts.
- Right side: Central bay with pediment, domed pavilions at each end of bridge.
- Left side: Central bay and end pavilions with pediments.

From Pulteney Bridge follow line of the road into
Argyle Street.

- Laid out by Thomas Baldwin, around 1775.
- Three blocks of plain housing.
- Mostly shop fronts at ground level.

From Argyle Street follow line of the road into
Laura Place.

- Laid out by Thomas Baldwin, around 1775.
- Octagon space formed by intersection of four house blocks and four roadways.
- Five-bay Palladian houses with rusticated ground level and columns (Fig. 81).
- Landscape planting.
- Central fountain.

From Laura Place follow line of the road into
Great Pulteney Street.

- Laid out by Thomas Baldwin, around 1775.
- Mainly blocks of three-bay plain housing (Fig. 82).
- North-side blocks have rusticated stonework at ground level. Also projecting central and end bays, triangular roof pediments, and Classical columns.
- South-side blocks have a mixture of rusticated stonework, central and end bays, pediments, and semi-circular windows at ground-floor level.

From Great Pulteney Street follow line of the road as far as the museum which provides the closing vista to the street (Fig. 83).

Fig. 81  Laura Place.

*Opposite above:* Fig. 82 Great Pulteney Street.

*Below:* Fig. 83 Closing vista, Great Pulteney Street.

Roman Baths in Britain

Ian D. Rotherham

The fascinating story of Britain's Roman Baths right up to the present day.

978 1 4456 0657 6

160 pages, 60 colour illustrations

Available from all good bookshops or order direct
from our website www.amberleybooks.com